D1714105

CONTENTS

BEST SWIMS IN ITALY

Sardinia Edition

FOREWORD

Welcome to our guide to Sardinia, a land that has captured our hearts and imagination over years of extensive travel. As impassioned adventurers, we've sought to encapsulate the island's essence and culture through our lens and descriptions. The photos and ideas within these pages aim to convey the multifaceted beauty, mystery and defining elements of this enchanting region.

Our hope is that you find enjoyment in these visual narratives and, more importantly, find inspiration to plan your own journey.

May you create lasting memories in this extraordinary island.

p67

Cupo D'orso

64

La Maddalena

Spargi

Rena Bianca

Santa Teresa di Gallura

Caprera

Piccolo Pevero

Li Cossi

Capo Testa

Rena Maiori

Baja Sardinia

Grande Pevero

Spiaggia del Principe

Asinara

La Marinedda

Palau

Porto Cervo

Capriccioli

La Celvia

La Pelosetta

Spiaggia Longa

Porto Pollo

Li Feruli

Porto Rotondo

Golfo Aranci

Li Junchi

Isola Rossa

I DELFINI

La Pelosa

Ezzi Mannu

Olbia

Tavolara Island

Molara Island

Castel Sardo

Cala Brandinchi

Porto Torres

Lu Impostu

Sassari

La Cinta

Budoni

p10

limestone cliffs

aquarium boats trip

Alghero

Berchida 7

Cala Liberotto

Lazzaretto

Cala Gonone

Cala Luna 13

Le Bombarde

Supramonte plateau

Cala Sisine

Gulf of Orosei

Cala Biriala

Mamoiada

Piscine di Venere

Orgosolo

Cala Mariolu 16

Fonni

Cala Golortizé

Santa Maria Navarrese

Mari Ermi

San Salvatore

Is Arutas

Cabras

Arbatax

Maimoni

Oristano

Lido di Orrì

San Giovanni di Sinis

Cea

best

P35 artists murals

Cala Domestica

Porto Flavia

Porto Cauli

Masua

Pan di Zucchero rock

Nebida

San Sperate

Cala di Monte Turno

Monteponi

Cala Sinzias

Fontanamare

Cagliari

Poetto

Carloforte

Santa Barbara Caves

Cala Pira

Punta Molentis

Carbonia

Mari Pintau

Porto Sa Ruxi

Porto Giunco

Campolongu

Cava Usai

31

Sant'Antioco

Teulada Marina

flamingos

P40

Porto Pino

Su Giudeu

Porto Scudo

Porto Pirastru

Cala Luna 13 caves

Porto Zafferano

The Americans' Beach

The map included in this guidebook outlines the itinerary spanning the diverse landscapes and stunning beaches of Sardinia. Beginning from the northeastern city of Olbia, the route meanders south along the prized Baunei Coast in the Gulf of Orosei, descending towards the dazzling blue beaches on the south eastern tip.

The itinerary then continues along the south coast reaching the islands of Sant'Antioco and Carloforte before tracing its way up the western side of the island towards the historic cities of Oristano and Alghero in the north.

The journey ventures to the island of Asinara in the northwest, then heads across the northen coast of Sardinia to the renowned Emerald Coast and La Maddalena Archipelago. Finally, it returns to Olbia, completing a memorable loop of Sardinia's most cherished sights.

INTRODUCTION

Sardinia unfolds along almost 2000 kilometres of coastline, a true paradise for beach enthusiasts. Choosing a beach here is a delightful experience, as the island's breathtaking waters effortlessly meet the high standards expected of tropical destinations, making it a fail-proof choice. This guidebook presents a curated list of Sardinia's most stunning beaches, bays, and coves. Vetted by seasoned travellers who've explored every nook of the island, these spots truly shine. All you have to do is pick your favourite and head there.

The island's allure extends well beyond its beaches; surprisingly, it's not predominantly linked to maritime traditions but pastoral ones. Shepherds and herdsmen populate the island's history and legends. Sardinia has generously contributed culturally unique offerings to the world, from delicious foods to traditional craftmanship. The island even boasts a distinct shepherding breed of dog, the Fonni shepherd dog – rugged and hardy, like the indomitable shepherds themselves.

As you delve into Sardinia's treasures, you'll encounter wild landscapes and unravel the depth of its cultural heritage. Explore the enduring nuraghe structures, ancient stone edifices scattered across the landscape, and the Domus de Janas, Neolithic tombs carved within large rock formations.

Watch out for the Mistral (*Maestrale* in Italian), a regular northwest wind, bringing relief from the summer heat for about 3 to 7 days at a time. Exercise caution when swimming on windy days, as the currents can be stronger. On such days, it's advisable to stay close to the shoreline.

As you explore Sardinia's beautiful beaches and coves, you'll definitely appreciate the freedom of access. The majority of these coastal wonders are free to the public, providing a cost-effective way to enjoy the island's natural beauty. While beach access is often free, be mindful of paid parking areas, which will always be clearly signposted.

You will need to hire a car to get around easily, as public transport is either lacking or erratic in most parts of the island. To reach Sardinia, you can travel by sea with shipping companies such as Grimaldi Lines (https://www.grimaldi-lines.com/it/), Moby (https://www.moby.it), Tirrenia (https://www.tirrenia.it) and Corsica Ferries (https://www.corsica-ferries.it) from major ports across Italy. Alternatively, you can fly with airlines that operate flights to Olbia and Cagliari airports.

Let's start our journey from Olbia, a bustling city in the northeast, likely your entry point via the airport or port.

FROM OLBIA TO VILLASIMIUS, FROM THE NORTH-EAST TO THE SOUTH- EAST

A short 20-minute drive south of Olbia leads to a stretch of coastline facing the iconic **island of Tavolara**, identified by its distinctive rocky crest and remarkable size. Tavolara, along with its neighbouring island **Molara**, forms a Marine Protected Area and offers opportunities for boat excursions and scuba diving.

Below: Tavolara, as seen from La Spiaggia del Dottore. On the following page: Cala Brandinchi "Little Tahiti".

Notable swimming spots in the vicinity include **La Spiaggia del Dottore, Le Tre Sorelle, Spiaggia di Porto Istana**, and the stunning **Spiaggia delle Vacche**, accessible by a stroll through lush vegetation. Amidst these beauties, however, the true high points are the twin beaches of **Cala Brandinchi** and **Lu Impostu**.

Cala Brandinchi, aptly named "Little Tahiti," lures

with its shimmering spectrum of blues and shallow, heavenly waters.

Brandinchi, with its rounded shoreline, is nestled in a secluded bay, sheltered from the wind. Though high season may draw crowds, it doesn't diminish the overall experience. Ample paid parking and beach stalls for food and drinks are available. As you take in all its beauty, the enchanting island of Tavolara rises on the left.

Lu Impostu, Cala Brandinchi's twin, symmetrically mirrors its length on the opposite side of a short promontory. Both beaches are complemented by natural water basins at their rear, creating ideal habitats for a diverse range of aquatic birds. Evolving shades of blue and fine sands make Lu Impostu nothing short of a tropical paradise.

Above: Tavolara as seen from Lu Impostu. Opposite: Lu Impostu's Caribbean palette.

Heading further south, you'll encounter the expansive stretch of white sandy beach known as **La Cinta**. This picturesque beach is almost three times the length of Brandinchi and Lu Impostu and, similarly, features shallow waters and enchanting hues of blue. On windy days, La Cinta becomes a perfect spot for kitesurfing

and various other watersports.

Budoni Beach is a long swathe of white sand with an adjacent pine forest. Its turquoise waters offer a shallow space for swimming. While it, too, can get breezy from time to time, Budoni provides a wonderful setting for sun, sea, and embracing the Sardinian atmosphere.

Among the authors' favourites, **Berchida** stands out due to its sheer size and pristine beauty, leaving a lasting impression on any beachgoer. This 5-kilometre white sandy beach is surrounded by imposing peaks covered in hardy Mediterranean scrub. A small watercourse named after the beach itself (*Riu Berchida*) and three water basins - two of which are within the **Biderosa Nature Reserve**, south of Berchida - add to its charm. Lucky visitors might even catch a glimpse of pink flamingo colonies, which temporarily inhabit this area (as well as other parts of the island) before migrating with changing weather.

On the following page: Berchida, as far as the eye can see. Close to the beach you will find archaeological sites from the nuraghic era and even the remains of a medieval village known as Rempellos.

✳ serene

Travelling southwards along the eastern coast of Sardinia, you'll come across **Cala Liberotto**. This small and serene spot, often free from large crowds, is framed by tall pine forests and sandy shores dotted with rocky outcrops. In the afternoon, the sea takes on mesmerising emerald hues.

On the following page: Cala Liberotto, blue and emerald. From the photo, the slightly rougher sand grains which make up this beach can be seen through the water. At the rear of the beach, the Sos Alinos pond enhances the natural scenery and serves as a sanctuary for aquatic birds.

The Gulf of Orosei, on the eastern coast of Sardinia, is renowned for its dramatic limestone cliffs jutting out at sea. This picturesque coastline is celebrated for having some of the island's most breathtaking bays and beaches (namely **Cala Luna**, **Cala Sisine**, **Piscine di Venere**, **Cala Mariolu**, and **Cala Goloritzé**). Ancient rivers run through harsh landscapes and cut through towering cliffs as they flow directly into the sea or create small lakes within the hidden recesses of the coves along the gulf. Boat tours depart regularly from the towns of **Cala Gonone**, **Santa Maria Navarrese**, and **Arbatax**. Private boat charters provide an exclusive option. In Cala Gonone and Arbatax, you'll find a variety of tour providers lining the harbour. Each offers different departure times, itineraries, and prices to match your preferences. As of 2024, adult prices begin at 50 euros per person. Adventurous individuals can opt for trekking routes over the cliffs that surround the coves, but be aware that such routes are physically very demanding.

Below: A further view of the cliffs in the Gulf of Orosei.

If you stop off in Cala Gonone, make sure to check out the local aquarium. **The Cala Gonone Aquarium**, though petite in size, makes for an enticing cultural stop. It houses a diverse collection of Mediterranean and tropical fish, including vibrant anemones, graceful jellyfish, and a resident turtle. A large tank sits right at the entrance, with some of the aquarium's larger fish, providing a thrilling introduction to the aquatic wonders within.

Below: Saddled seabream (called occhiate in Italian) along the Baunei coast, in the Gulf of Orosei.

Cala Luna is accessible by trekking or boat. It is appreciated for its sandy shores and diverse marine life, which includes saddled seabream (*occhiate*), garfish, and damselfish. This cove features mesmerising caves and a brook flowing into the sea. The caves exude a primordial energy, inviting curious travellers to explore their distinctive formations and the interplay of light and shadow within.

Below: Cala Luna's sparkling waters. This will be your first stop on boat tours departing from Cala Gonone. Next: inside one of the "prehistoric" caves which pierce the northern side of Cala Luna.

snorkeling

Cala Sisine, south of Cala Luna, boasts a 500-metre-long pebble beach with rounded stones in various shades, and is ideal for snorkelling. This particular cove is known for the ever-changing hues of its waters influenced by the sun and clouds. It is accessible by trekking or sea.

South of Cala Sisine are **Venus's Pools**, or *Piscine di Venere* in Italian. The colour of the sea here jostles between emerald and teal. It is accessible only by private speedboat or a challenging trek for the physically fit.

Below: Venus' s Pools, as seen from the boat.

Cala Biriala is a small beach, bejewelled with white pebbles and enclosed by limestone cliffs. Whether arriving by boat or opting for a nature-infused trek, this beach beckons as a peaceful retreat.

Cala Mariolu is a coastal masterpiece embellished with oval-shaped pebbles of varying tones, from pure white to pale yellow and blush pink. The astonishingly clear water reveals a seabed of white limestone, pebble, and rock. In the local dialect, *mariolu* means thief and was used to describe the monk seals that used to inhabit these waters. Local fishermen believed the seals were stealing fish from their nets and sadly, this perception led to the hunting and extinction of seals in this region. Cala Mariolu's waters abound with seabream, providing a chance for an up-close encounter with these amiable creatures. Encircled by towering cliffs and adorned with sea-carved grottos, this beach epitomises the spectacular beauty of Sardinia's coastline. Note that trekking to this cove is recommended for expert hikers due to the challenging terrain.

Below: Cala Mariolu as seen when you approach from the sea. US-based website "The World's 50 Best Beaches" lists Cala Mariolu as the second most beautiful beach in the world in its 2024 ranking. This spectacular cove has made an appearance in a number of different international listings and keeps securing top spots year after year.

On the following page: The levigated pebbles in Cala Mariolu (left) and a detail of one of its sea caves (right). Its unique morphological features coupled with the pristine quality of its waters, help create a truly unparalled sight.

Cala Goloritzé stands out for its towering pinnacle reaching 143 metres into the sky. The beach, only accessible by a challenging two-hour trek, boasts enchanting blue waters uncannily resembling the colour of sportsdrinks.

Above: Goloritzé and its iconic pinnacle. On the next page: The electric shades of blue around Golortizè.

You may come across wild donkeys and goats on your trek down, as the animals often stop to drink at a spring close to the shore. The beach itself is scattered with finely smoothed white pebbles.

Descending from the coastal beauties of the Gulf of Orosei, the journey inland unveils a rich tapestry of tradition and heritage. The eastern part of the island has a strong, staunch identity, reflected in its inland towns. Moving away from the sun-kissed beaches, the landscape transitions to hilly mountainous terrain, where time seems to move at its own unhurried pace. **Orgosolo**, one such town, stands as a living testament to what Sardinia was in bygone days. It is particularly known for its vibrant murals scattered throughout the town, depicting stories of politics and society.

While the locals may seem reserved at first, they quickly embrace visitors, revealing their warmth and generosity. The town, however, strictly adheres to traditional gender roles, with women refraining from leaving their homes after dusk, while only men are seen on the streets at night.

The town thrives on local traditions intertwined with religious practices that take place throughout the year. Orgosolo takes great pride in its traditional costumes, culinary treasures, and cherished recipes. Notably, the town has a tongue-in-cheek enmity with neighbouring towns and what were once rival clans, adding an intriguing layer to its storied past.

The neighbouring town of **Mamoiada** holds a special charm with its quaint Mediterranean mask museum. Despite its small size, the museum is a little cultural gem. Mamoiada's town centre also provides a snapshot of Sardinia's rich heritage. Be sure to check their website https://www.museomaschere.it for the most up-to-date information on opening hours and admission prices.

On the previous page: Two political murals along the streets in Orgosolo.

On the following page: A mouthwatering Sardinian dessert called seada (seadas in the plural) consisting of fried savoury dough filled with pecorino cheese, and lemon peel, topped with either sugar or honey.

In the central part of Sardinia, in the region known as **Barbagia**, the tradition of mask-making takes centre stage during public celebrations akin to a carnival. Masks reflect both human and animal characters. Animal figures, like the ox, the deer and the donkey, perform alongside human figures representing herders or other traditional characters. Among the most memorable are the **Mamuthones**, donning black wooden masks, sheepskins, and hefty bells, accompanied by the **Issohadores**, whose role it is to lasso them.

In the proximity of Mamoiada and Orgosolo lies **Fonni**—a town known for its distinctive breed of dog, the Fonni Shepherd Dog. These sizable canines, characterized by their large stature, dark grey or black shaggy fur, and striking orange/brown eyes, embody loyalty and protection. Serving as formidable guardians for their owners, flocks, and livestock, these dogs are not only vigilant protectors but also dedicated workers, carrying out their duties with commitment. Resilient to harsh weather conditions and well-suited to outdoor life, the Fonni Shepherd Dog plays a vital role in preserving the island's rich pastoral heritage.

The "Little Green Train" is a narrow-gauge railway originally used for transporting coal and minerals. This quaint historical train takes passengers on a picturesque journey from **Arbatax** across the **Gennargentu massif**. Boarding vintage green carriages, travellers can anticipate breathtaking views as the train crosses looming bridges spanning gorges and valleys, evocative of scenes from classic Western films.

If you are a nature enthusiast and hiker, this mountain range and surrounding rugged landscapes, should be of particular interest to you. Gennargentu is, in fact, the island's highest mountain range and is famous for its deep gorges - with **Gorropu** being one of Europe's deepest canyons - and the **Supramonte plateau** with its unique plant and animal life.

On the following page: The "Little Green Train" crossing the isolated interior landscapes across the Gennargentu massif. The train operates several routes throughout the island, with the Arbatax to

Gairo route being a recommended option.

The train makes several stops along the way, including at the abandoned town of **Gairo Vecchio**. For those eager to explore further, excursions into the surrounding hills reveal stories of local groups who once roamed these hills and used them as hideouts for kidnapping and ransom activities—an intriguing historical anecdote. Additional excursions on foot through the Gennargentu mountain complex will take you across imposing peaks and awe-inspiring lands that have endured the test of time. Be sure to visit the official website for the most current information and prices at http://www.treninoverde.com

More than just a mode of transport, the "Little Green Train" is a journey through the heart of Sardinia's untouched interior, completing a full circle of exploration as it returns to Arbatax.

Below: A herd of goats looks for shade among the trees in Gairo Vecchio. The village was completely abandoned following a flood in the 1950s.

As you head back towards the coastline, we highly recommend **Lido di Orrì** for some of the best swims in the area. Located south of Arbatax, Orrì is an easily accessible beach with clear, shallow waters and fine sandy shores. Backed by a line of beach bars, it extends as far as the eye can see. Distinctive grey rock formations emerge from the water along the shoreline, adding character to the beach while providing inviting spots to sit and enjoy the tranquil surroundings.

Below: Orri's rounded boulders along the shore.

Just south of Orrì, two vivid red sea stacks rise proudly from the cerulean waters. The beach overlooking them, known as **Cea**, offers accessible comfort with well-maintained facilities and ample parking. Rental options like canoes and pedalos are a boon.

Below: The red sea stacks in Cea are made of porphyry and illuminate at sunset, offering their most impressive display.

Sardinia has a rich archaeological heritage marked by thousands of **Nuraghes**, ancient stone structures dispersed across the landscape. These structures resemble stone towers, with some being well-preserved while others exist as scattered blocks of stone. Visitors can explore these ancient constructions alongside other intriguing elements, including **menhirs**—tall standing stones that add to the island's ancient charm. Across Sardinia, you'll come across signposts for

"**Domus de Janas**," indicating rocky outcrops which are actually prehistoric tombs. These sites are steeped in folklore, believed to be the haunts of mythical female figures known as the Janas, who were once considered guardians of these places. The Janas are integral to the island's traditions.

Below: The S'Ortali 'e Su Monti nuraghe, in Tortolì. Not far from this nuraghe, lies a whitewashed country church atop a hill dedicated to Saint Salvatore. A short 2-minute drive will take you there. We recommend going at sunset for a magical experience.

On the southern coast of Arbatax lies **Porto Frailis**. This beach has fine, golden sand and turquoise waters, creating a very relaxed atmosphere surrounded by rugged cliffs and natural rock formations.

Cala di Monte Turno: This bay is characterized by a distinctive hillock extending into the sea at its northern end, with emerald green waters surrounded by luscious Mediterranean shrubs and plants.

Below: A sunny day in Porto Frailis. Easy parking and sheltered conditions make it ideal for families.

Cala Pira: This beach features powder-blue waters, sandy dunes, and a 16th-century lookout turret at its northern end. The sand's varying coral composition may give it a subtle pinkish hue. The uninhabited **island of Serpentera** is visible across the water. Convenient parking is just a short stroll from the sea.

Cala Sinzias: Offering wide-open spaces and panoramic vistas, this beach is dotted with delicate white lilies belonging to the **Pancratium maritimum** species – a familiar sight on many of the island's beaches.

Above: a cluster of lilies sprouting from the sand.

Heading south along the eastern coast, you'll reach the town of **Villasimius**, known for its vibrant coastal waters that unveil a vivid Powerade-like intensity (when pronouncing the word Villasimìus, stress falls on the final "i").

Held within the sheltered embrace of a granite quarry, **Punta Molentis** is accessible by a boat tour departing from the marina in Villasimius or by car along a dirt track. Boat tours often include a delightful lunch with locally sourced seafood and a visit to the nearby **Cabbage Island** (*Isola dei Cavoli*). This island is actually a nature reserve known for its lighthouse and a sunken sculpture of the Madonna, placed on the seabed in 1979 to safeguard seafarers. The waters in Punta Molentis paint a spectrum of colours, transitioning from crystal clear to electric blue.

Porto Giunco is a personal favourite, set in a natural landscape that includes a lake—a cherished nesting ground for flamingos—and a large salt pan. All around are green promontories that extend over land and sea, creating a diverse range of ecosystems. A 16th-century Spanish turret atop one of these hillocks serves as a historical lookout post, offering panoramic views of the surrounding coast.

Cava Usai, lying to the right of the 16th-century turret in Porto Giunco, was once a quarry. Today, it's a picturesque cascade of granite blocks lining the cliffs and descending into the sea. With crystal-clear waters and views of the protected marine area, Cava Usai is a popular destination for swimming and exploration.

On the following page: Friendly saddled sea bream will swim around you in most beaches unfazed by human presence.

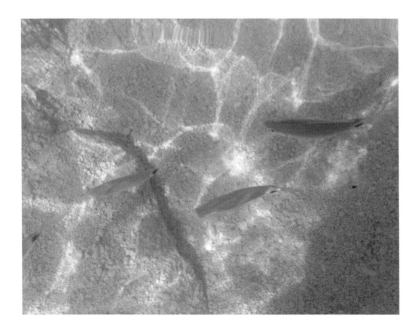

Campulongu, just a short drive from the port in Villasimius, is a long, narrow shoreline overlooking shallow, crystalline waters. It's an in-demand destination, especially during peak seasons. Arriving early is recommended to secure a spot and convenient parking for an overall delightful beach experience.

Mari Pintau, located halfway between Cagliari and Villasimius, is a secluded pebble beach. A brief stroll through the Mediterranean scrub is needed to reach this beach after parking your car. Water shoes are recommended. This is a peaceful bay, surrounded by rolling hills.

Porto Sa Ruxi, a trio of coves seamlessly joined by natural rock formations, beckons you with its fine sandy shores and inviting turquoise waters. You'll walk along paths lined with junipers, myrtles and other Mediterranean shrubs to get here, and, once you arrive, you'll find convenient kiosks and rentals for beach equipment.

* * *

FROM CAGLIARI TO ASINARA, FROM THE SOUTH TO THE NORTH-WEST

Cagliari is the capital city of Sardinia. Its historic city centre, with a strong medieval character, is perched on a hill. The old town is surrounded by bastions and is embellished by a castle, towers, and aristocratic buildings. Around the city, salt pans and calm pools of water offer opportunities for bird watching and hiking, making Cagliari a diverse destination worth exploring.

Poetto: Extending across the bay between Quartu Sant'Elena and Cagliari, Poetto is a large sandy beach known for its ease of access, services, and proximity to the city centre. Occasionally, dolphins can be spotted in its crystal-clear waters, too.

San Sperate: Located north of Cagliari, the village of San Sperate is a place where local artists, deeply connected to their homeland, open their doors to visitors, sharing their talents and stories. One distinctive feature of San Sperate is its vibrant murals, which grace the sides of numerous buildings.

Su Giudeu beach, known for its shallow waters, is very family-friendly. During low tide, you can even wade through the water to a small islet close to the coast. A large pond behind the beach hosts migratory birds seasonally. The sea displays changing hues depending on the time of day, and the beach is surrounded by soft, golden sand dunes.

On the following page: An artist's house in San Sperate. If you can, pay a visit to artist Pinuccio Sciola's Sound Garden, an open air museum where megalithic sculptures produce incredible sounds. For more information visit https://www.psmuseum.it

The Teulada marina serves as a small harbour where local and touristic vessels dock. Head here for tours that provide access to some of the finest, and otherwise inaccessible, coves along this coastline. Some of them are within restricted areas, such as military shooting ranges, meaning that visitors can only tread the first few meters of the shoreline. Here is a list of some of the coves you will have the opportunity to swim in, subject to the discretion of the boat excursion leaders:

The Americans' Beach, or *Spiaggia degli Americani* in Italian, is the initial stop on a westward sea excursion. Though not large, this pristine beach is nestled amidst dense vegetation.

Porto Pirastu is a secluded bay, enveloped by a verdant landscape. White sand and shallow waters are its defining features.

Porto Scudo is a tranquil bay enclosed by green hills. It's not uncommon to encounter cattle on the shore, where they can be found leisurely basking in the sun. The water has a mesmerizing turquoise hue – a real treat for the eyes.

Right: The colour of the sea in Porto Scudo.

Porto Zafferano is within a military base and only accessible in the summer months. It has incredibly shallow waters and soft fine sand. The shoreline is protected by a natural barrier of delicately white sand dunes. Sailing west along the coast, you'll reach the southernmost point of Sardinia (named Capo Teulada), marked by a tall rocky façade proudly standing out at sea.

Below: the shallow sandy seabed in Porto Zafferano (top) and Capo Teulada (bottom).

Porto Pino is a 6km bay, known for its extensive sandy shoreline. The water here is very shallow for a considerable distance. On the western side, you'll find dense pine forests, while the eastern end features a large area covered by tall dunes known as **Is Arenas Biancas**.

Please note that these dunes are located within a military shooting range and are accessible only during the summer. At the back of the bay, there are five large bodies of water, some used for farming mussels and eels. The area has many shops, restaurants, and hotels.

Left: Shallow waters in Porto Pino, with the Is Arenas Biancas dunes visible at the far end of the beach.

Off the south-western coast of Sardinia, lie the two neighbouring islands of **Sant'Antioco** and **Carloforte**. Sant'Antioco, connected to Sardinia by a substantial bridge, stands out as the larger of the two islands. The main town is a charming maritime village which goes by the same name. The island has a reputation for exceptional fish dishes, highlighting the strong maritime traditions in this area. Its relaxed atmosphere is more akin to a tranquil fishing village than anything else. The main town may be busier, especially in the evening when people head out for dinner and a stroll along the main street. Yet, it is overall quieter than mainland Sardinia. Having a car is essential for getting around, especially since some bays may require navigating a greater number of dirt tracks compared to other beaches in Sardinia.

Above: A sauté of mussels at a fish restaurant in the main town of Sant'Antioco. We can recommend " Ittiturismo Cooperativa - I Due Fratelli" seafood restaurant in the heart of the main town. Their website is https://www.ittiturismoiduefratelli.com

On the following page: The striking polychromy of the sea in Portixeddu beach, Sant'Antioco. Wearing water shoes is recommended at this pebble beach as the sand is covered with rounded stones that continue into the sea for the first few metres, making it quite challenging to walk barefoot.

Some of the best beaches in Sant'Antioco are:

Maladroxia Beach: A popular sandy beach with

transparent waters, perfect for swimming and snorkelling. You will surely enjoy the convenience of nearby restaurants and bars.

Spiaggia Grande: This is a roomy beach with fine sand and gentle waters, making it a family-friendly choice, all topped off by beautiful vistas and close-by amenities.

Coaquaddus Beach: Recognized for its reddish rocks and pristine waters, drawing swimmers and snorkelling enthusiasts alike, this beach offers a more secluded atmosphere compared to some of its counterparts.

The island of **Carloforte**, accessible by ferry from Portovesme, has a distinctive role in Sardinia's history. Historically, it became a settlement for groups of sailors from Genoa, and traces of Genoese culture endure to this day. Carloforte stands out for its architectural style, more akin to Liguria than traditional Sardinian design, showcasing the diverse influences that have shaped its character over time. As you stroll though the streets of the main town, be sure to visit some of the churches. They exude an authentic atmosphere with their small size and heartfelt votive art, speaking to the strong connection between the fishermen and seafarers, and their faith.

For some of the best swims on the island, head to **La Bobba Beach** and **Cala Vinagra**, known for their clear waters and beautiful scenery. **Spiaggia del Giunco** is also a popular choice for beachgoers, with fine sandy shores and transparent waters. Otherwise, head to **Cala**

Fico, accessible by boat, or **Spiaggia di Guidi**, with its baby-blue waters - a great place to soak up the sun and sea.

The southwest region of Sardinia, called **Sulcis**, is renowned for its rugged wilderness, beautiful beaches, and the well-preserved remnants of mining villages from the past.

Sardinia's Southwest has a rich mining history, with numerous mines currently turned into museums and listed as **UNESCO heritage sites**. Interestingly, **Carbonia** was a mining town built during fascist times – many industrial towns, in fact, were established across Italy during Mussolini's tenure. They often bore women's names and were designed to attract workmen and their families to newly built industrial areas. Carbonia, as the Italian name suggests (*carbone* = coal), was a coal mining town. One of the main mines in the area is known as **Serbariu**.

On the previous page: A view of Carbonia's main square and belfry. Erected between 1937 and 1938, this town is a prime example of fascist architecture.

Below: The remains of machinery and facilities used for processing extracted ore at the former San Giovanni mines.

The nearby **Monteponi Mining District**, with its striking red soil, is remembered for its lead and zinc mining operations in the 1900s. The hillocks surrounding the mine, with their red-brown colour, resemble the arid interior landscapes of Australia.

On the following page: I Fanghi Rossi (Red Mud) are an accumulation of iron oxides, a by-product of the zinc extraction process in the Monteponi area.

Inland, visitors can explore a series of **cave systems**, most notably the **Santa Barbara caves**, with their exquisite stalagmites, stalactites, and a unique underground environment.

Particularly appreciated among the beaches in this area is **Fontanamare**. This 4km beach is known for its openness to the sea, which can often result in windy conditions. Despite the lack of natural barriers, it offers enjoyable swimming experiences on calm days, showcasing its rugged beauty. Driving north along the coastline from Fontanamare, you'll encounter the remnants of **the Nebida mines**, devoted to the extraction of lead and zinc. Still visible today are the outer walls of the extraction plant and two chimney stacks. Please note that the coastal road heading north winds along steep cliffs, demanding cautious driving.

Heading ever northwards, you'll reach the former mining district of **Masua**, known for the **Pan di Zucchero rock** - an iconic sea stack named after Rio de Janeiro's Pao de Açucar. Three smaller sea stacks scattered across the sea here add to this truly unique landscape.

Below: Masua and the famed Pan di Zucchero sea stack at sunset. This imposing rock formation is 133 metres tall and can be reached by boat or canoe. Much loved by climbers, this unique geological feature is made of pure limestone. Two of the smaller, neighbouring sea stacks are named s'Augusteri and Il Morto.

Masua and Porto Cauli beaches are situated amidst

greenish rocky cliffs, which, in turn, give the sea a green hue. The sunset is particularly spectacular in this area.

Above: The peculiar green hues of the rocks and cliffs in and around Masua and Porto Cauli.

A 10-minute drive from Masua takes you to **Porto Flavia**, the famous extraction complex perched on a cliff. Lead, zinc, and silver used to be extracted here. Today, visitors can explore this mining site and tunnel system, which culminates in a breathtakingly panoramic drop overlooking the sea. Just beneath the tunnel of Porto Flavia, you'll find its small homonymous beach.

As you continue north along the coastline, you'll come to **Cala Domestica**. This fjord-like cove is surrounded by sand dunes, so you'll have to walk along a boardwalk designed to protect them before accessing the beach.

On your left, you'll see the remains of the miners' work quarters still standing today. Limestone cliffs encircle the cove on both sides.

Below: La Caletta, a secluded bay to the right of Cala Domestica.

If you are looking for an alternative day trip to the beach, inland from the coast, Sardinia is replete with a variety of stunning waterfalls and mountain tracks.

As you enter into the **Sinis Peninsula** in the north, make sure to pay a visit to **the Tharros archaeological site**, which overlooks beautiful beaches with aquamarine waters. This evocative site on the promontory is a layered testament to the history of different peoples and cultures. Particularly harrowing is the **tophet**, a burial site possibly associated with ritual ceremonies that included children.

The small village of **San Giovanni di Sinis**, situated

along the Sinis peninsula, and its homonymous church are unmissable. This **11th-century Byzantine church** exudes a timeless and sacred atmosphere found in only the most exceptional of places.

Above: The San Giovanni Church, with its unassuming exterior made of blocks of sandstone, holds a special place in the hearts of those who have set foot in it.

The seawater on this side of the island stays cool and refreshing throughout the summer, but that shouldn't deter you from visiting the enchanting trio of beaches called **Maimoni, Mari Ermi**, and **Is Arutas**. These one-of-a-kind beaches are covered in precious grains of pink, white, and light gray quartz, a unique feature on the island. The water near the shoreline displays Caribbean-like iridescence. Please note that the water level in Is Arutas deepens quite rapidly, whereas Maimoni and

Mari Ermi have a more gradual depth increase.

On this page: Mari Ermi on a stormy early September morning. The currents along these beaches may bring the occasional jellyfish close to shore. Typically, they'll be Mediterranean Cassiopea jellyfish, harmless and colourful, often called "fried egg" jellyfish. Below: The grains of quartz that make up the beach in Mari Ermi.

Above: The iridescent sea in Is Arutas.

A short drive from these beaches is the town of **San Salvatore**, known for being one of the preferred locations for spaghetti westerns in the 60s and 70s. Visitors can explore its unique low-lying architecture and rustic charm by strolling through its narrow alleys.

On the following page: The village of San Salvatore as seen from its main square on a late summer afternoon.

Crossing the bridge over **Cabras Pond** you will enter into the town of **Cabras**. Here, the **Giovanni Marongiu Museum** houses the so-called **Giants**. These are life-size stone sculptures of warriors and athletes, a truly unequaled archaeological discovery retrieved from the Mont'e Prama necropolis, dating back 3,000 years.

If you feel up for a dive into the past, a 10-minute drive will take you to the larger town of **Oristano** with its beautiful historical centre. Here, a unique folk festival called "Sartiglia" takes place on the last Sunday of Carnival and on Shrove Tuesday. It features a procession of 120 horsemen and a horse race. If you're in the Oristano area duing Carnival, it's definitely worth seeing.

To savour local specialties, try pasta with bottarga (dried mullet eggs) paired with a high-quality local wine, such as vinaccia.

Journey north to **Alghero**, a remarkable city with a

unique blend of Sardinian and Catalan influences. The streets and buildings are permeated by shades of ochre, lending a warm Mediterranean charm to its historical centre. When you visit, make sure to try the local paella and take a stroll along the imposing bastions that run along its perimeter. Historically, the coast of Alghero has been a flourishing site for the extraction and manufacturing of red coral.

Above: Alghero seen from the seafront promenade. Make sure to avoid some of the tourist trap restaurants in the historical city centre by reading up-to-date online reviews on Google. On the next page: Le Bombarde beach and its shallow, child-

friendly waters.

A few kilometres from the Alghero area, **Le Bombarde**

and **Lazzaretto beaches** are recognized for their exceptional beauty. Bring water shoes when visiting Le Bombarde, as there are a great many emerging rocks along the shoreline. This particular beach is framed on both ends by reddish rocky outcrops and surrounded, at its rear, by a verdant pine forest.

Just to the north, is a regional park and a protected marine area. For a unique day out, visit **Neptune's Caverns**, where you can admire unique rock formations and even an underground lake.

On the north-western tip of Sardinia, the impressive **La Pelosa beach** has the accolade of being among the most beautiful beaches in Italy and in Europe. Lying not far from the fishing village of Stintino, it is unanimously appreciated for its shallow waters and Caribbean-like colours. Keep in mind that access is restricted, requiring advance online booking. From June to October, la Pelosa Beach accepts bookings through its official website, https://spiaggialapelosa.it typically allowing up to 1,500 entries per day. The entry fee is around 3.50 euros per person.

Alternatively, its smaller sister beach, **La Pelosetta**, offers an access point for those willing to swim along the coastline to reach the more renowned La Pelosa beach.

On the following page: La Pelosa beach on a sunny day. On the horizon just ahead, lies the island of Asinara. To the left, is an islet called Isola Piana, close enough to swim to. The fortuitous geographical layout of this beach and the surrounding islands contributes to its calmness even during adverse weather conditions.

On the following page: Two views of La Pelosa on an overcast day - arguably an even more beautiful and mystical sight in bad weather. Clearly visibile in the top photo is the 16th-century tower known as Torre della Pelosa.

Opposite La Pelosa lies the uninhabited island of **Asinara**. Formerly a high-security prison, it is now a national park where donkey colonies thrive. The island has experienced a rich and varied history dating back to ancient times, but it is in the modern period that it has undergone significant transformations. Initially used as a pasture for animals, the island became a penal colony in the 19th century and later a place of exile and detention for war prisoners in the early 20th century. Over time, it also became a centre for the detention of criminals and mafia bosses. Today, with rugged landscapes and secluded beaches, Asinara provides an authentic off-the-beaten-path experience in Sardinia.

Above: Asinara on a calm, clear day. An abandoned turret and stone shack complete the picture.

* * *

FROM ASINARA TO GOLFO ARANCI, FROM THE NORTH-WEST TO THE NORTH-EAST

Reminiscent of the beautiful trio of beaches in Cabras, **Ezzi Mannu beach** (just a 20-minute drive east from La Pelosa) is covered in small, white quartz pebbles. This 2-kilometre stretch of land offers pale turquoise waters and is occasionally impacted by winds that bring seagrass to the shore - a natural occurrence on many beaches in Sardinia. The occasional presence of seagrass on the shore is a sign of a healthy and ecologically diverse coastal environment. Accessible via a dirt road, this spot is truly stunning.

Heading eastward leads to **Porto Torres**, a town serving ferries to Corsica and mainland Italy. Once a lively town, it now appears deserted and lacks significant options for entertainment, accommodation, and dining.

Sassari, on the other hand, is the second-largest city on the island after Cagliari. Its refined historical centre, full of elegant old buildings and churches, provides a pleasant break from seaside activities. Sassari offers a variety of shops, businesses, and entertainment spots, although it's not a bustling tourist hotspot. One notable landmark is **St. Nicholas's Cathedral**, also called **Sassari Cathedral**, with its mixture of architectural styles and inviting light-coloured stone.

On the following page: Sassari Cathedral is the largest church in Sardinia, with its imposing 30-metre-high façade.

Stop off at the town of **Castelsardo**, perched on a promontory with an exquisite view of the entire **Gulf of Asinara**. Its unique location makes it stand out in the whole of Sardinia. The town has a characteristic historical centre developing vertically towards the dominating 12th-century **Doria Castle**, which marks the town's highest point. The narrow alleyways, similar to those of medieval towns in central Italy, add to its strongly medieval character. Notably, the town is home to a beautiful **cathedral** named after **Saint Anthony Abbott**. Overall, Castelsardo has a distinct charm that sets it apart from other towns on the island.

As you drive to Castelsardo, be sure to make a brief photo stop at **Elephant's Rock**. This unusual trachyte formation sits surprisingly close to the road and earned its name because the elements sculpted it across the eons to resemble an elephant and its trunk. It's a fascinating natural wonder worth capturing during your journey.

Below: Elephant's Rock, on a sunny afternoon.

As you move eastwards from Castelsardo, you will find an incredibly long stretch of sand which goes by different names. Nominally, it's called **the Bay of Mimosas Beach**. This 3-kilometre swathe of land then takes the name of **Li Junchi**, and further on, **Li Feruli**. Golden yellow grains of sand, vast open spaces, clear and swiftly deepening waters are its hallmark. What's more, this wild, solitary beach is embellished by golden sand dunes and sweetly-scented Mediterranean shrubs. However, be mindful of strong currents, so it's advisable to check environmental conditions before venturing into the sea.

A 20-minute drive eastwards will take you to **Isola Rossa**, formerly a thriving fishing village turned tourist resort. Set on a promontory facing a distinctive red-coloured rocky outcrop at sea, the town derives its name from this feature. Isola Rossa exudes a relaxed atmosphere, far from the chaotic, tourist-heavy town centres found in places like Villasimius and other locations along the southeastern coast. This postcard-perfect town has a **16th-century Aragonese Tower** and a marina, which welcomes boaters and local fishermen alike. Nearby, the stunning **Spiaggia Longa** features fine sand and baby-blue waters with rounded pebbles, making water shoes advisable. Shallow waters make this beach conveniently family-friendly.

On the following page: Unmistakable red rocks and a characteristic fjord in the northern part of Isola Rossa.

Close to the town of Isola Rossa is **La Marinedda**, a beautiful beach that caters to various amenities for beachgoers. Easily accessible and ideal for families and water sports enthusiasts, this beach boasts turquoise waters and fine sand, providing a delightful setting for a day by the sea.

If you're up for a trek across an almost lunar, extraterrestrial landscape, head to **Li Cossi Cove**. Park your car at a distance and continue on foot. The trek will be amply repaid by the unique setting of this cove. Along the route, the incredible rock formations create small pools, and the water displays a range of colours from green to turquoise to sky blue. You'll be hard-pressed to find a more unique beach than this. There's more than one route to access it, and one of them traces the course of a river which runs through the mountains. The sandy shore is equipped with a beach bar. Trekking to the cove is safe, but you'll need appropriate footwear.

Below: A view of Li Cossi from atop a stone staircase that leads to the eastern side of the cove. On the following page: A striking rock formation along the route.

This part of the northern coastline is called **Costa Paradiso** (Paradise Coast), and the name says it all. The overwhelming presence of granite and trachyte creates oneiric shapes and configurations, offering a unique spot for wildlife and a high concentration of biodiversity. It is not uncommon to see families of boars leisurely strolling along the streets and carparks snuffling around for food.

Head eastwards to the beach of **Rena Maiori,** where unfettered nature predominates. Here you can combine walks in the Mediterranean shrub and pine forests with a delightful dip in the sea. This white sandy beach is a favoured location for film and advertising and is particularly mesmerising at sunset. The jagged rocks to the left create a dramatic backdrop, and the sea looks like liquid mercury as the sun loses its intensity late in the afternoon. Streaks of pink sand, attributed to ground minerals as well as seashell and coral particles, contribute an additional touch of beauty to this already enchanting beach.

Below: Rena Maiori on a late summer afternoon. On the following page: Pink particles streak the sand in Rena Maiori.

As you move ever eastwards and upwards, you will

come across the maritime town of **Santa Teresa di Gallura**, overlooking the Straits of Bonifacio, where ships depart for Corsica. The most beautiful beach in this area is **Rena Bianca**, which can get very crowded in summer. Having said this, its almost impalpable white sand and tropical-looking waters will make up for any discomfort caused by crowded conditions during the summer season. You'll forget you're in the midst of a plethora of beach umbrellas.

The nearby headland of **Capo Testa** is also worth a visit, with its majestic granite cliffs and a lighthouse that provide panoramic views of the coastline. Capo Testa is often cited as one of the most beautiful coastal areas in the world. On the western side of the promontory, lies what is known as Valle della Luna (Valley of the Moon), a trail that winds through granite rocks towering above passersby, creating lunar-like formations. Several coves open up at the end of each path. This valley was and still is frequented by a hippie community, who call it their home.

Below: Rena Bianca during peak season still retains its charm and enjoyability.

Between **Santa Teresa di Gallura** and **Palau** is the well-known beach of **Porto Pollo**, a hotspot for water sport lovers, hosting international competitions too. Water sport schools, which include options for children, abound in this area. Regularly swept by the Mistral wind, Porto Pollo is particularly well-suited for various water activities, making it a popular destination for enthusiasts and competitors alike.

The coastline leading up to Palau is dotted with rocky coves and cosy, unspoilt beaches - one secluded gem among these is **Cala Martinella**. This area marks the beginning of the more high-end, exclusive side of the island, with privileged neighborhoods and gated communities, giving the area a quietly elitist feel.

Above: Cala Martinella, far from the madding crowd.

Palau serves as a vital connection between Sardinia and **the Maddalena archipelago**, offering daily ferry links. The town has an old historic centre interspersed with traditional buildings. Left of the city, stands the 19th-century fort of **Monte Altura**, providing spellbinding views over the surrounding area and the sea. To the right of Palau, is **Bear's Rock**, a granite formation similar to Elephant's Rock near Castelsardo. This stone structure, predictably resembling a giant bear, requires a small fee to be visited.

The Maddalena archipelago is a group of islands off the northeastern coast of Sardinia, with the main island being **La Maddalena** itself - the largest among them. Other notable islands include **Caprera**, **Santo Stefano**,

Spargi, **Budelli**, **Santa Maria**, **Razzoli**, and several minor islets. Designated as a **national park** in 1994, the archipelago boasts a variety of pristine beaches and coves. Exploring these gems is best done by boat, and guided boat tours are available, departing from the main island of Sardinia and the archipelago itself. Below is a list of some of the most inspiring beaches in the area.

Starting from the beaches on the island of La Maddalena, we can recommend **Cala Spalmatore** in the northeast. This secluded cove offers sheltered swims on a windy day, with shallow waters and a freshwater pond in the back. Warm-coloured granite rocks frame this small yet peaceful beach on either side.

Above: Cala Spalmatore on a cloudy, breezy day.

In the northwest, **Bassa Trinità** is a fine sandy beach

surrounded by unspoilt dunes, making it ideal for the whole family. The waters here are calm, sheltered, and great for snorkelling.

Below: The dunes in Bassa Trinità.

A bridge connects the island of La Maddalena with the island of **Caprera**. Caprera is a verdant place covered in aromatic pine forests and typical Mediterranean shrubs. Noteworthy beaches include **Spiaggia del Relitto**, or Wreckage Beach, on the southernmost tip in the east. This is possibly the most Caribbean-looking among the beaches in the archipelago, alongside Cala Coticcio in the north. It derives its name from the remains of an ancient sunken ship, which are still visible today, scantily emerging from the white sand along the shoreline.

Below: The wooden frame of the ship's bow is visible in the bottom left corner of this picture.

Cala Coticcio, also dubbed "Little Tahiti" because of the brilliant colour of its waters, is an excellent spot for snorkelling. This cove can only be accessed via an hour-long guided trekking tour, leading across a rocky landscape dotted with low-lying Mediterranean vegetation. Booking is required, and there is a fee (ca. 25 euro p.p.).

Caprera was the final residence of Garibaldi, and his former home is now a museum. One of the coves on the island, known as **Cala Garibaldi**, is dedicated to him. Just north of Cala Garibaldi, there are other secluded, wild inlets - one particularly beautiful spot is named

Cala Serena.

Opposite Caprera, on the main island of Sardinia, lies the town of **Baja Sardinia**, developed in the 1960s during the construction boom along the northeastern coast. This town serves as a departure point for boats, vessels, and private tours offering excursions to the nearby archipelago, along with opportunities for whale-watching and dolphin-watching. Baja Sardinia has two particularly stunning beaches: **Cala Battistoni** and **Cala Trimonti**.

A guided boat tour or private boat transfer will take you to **Isola Spargi**, the neighbouring smaller island east of La Maddalena. Two exceptional places on this island are **Cala Granara** and **Cala Corsara** to the south. These cyan coves with soft sandy shores and shallow waters, are a real treat for the senses.

On the next page: Cala Granara's tropical colour palette.

Head north to **Isola Budelli** and **Isola Santa Maria**. The highlight of Isola Budelli is the so-called **Pink Beach**, *Spiaggia Rosa*, which guided boat tours do not stop at, citing environmental reasons. Isola Santa Maria is a small and barely inhabited island. Ensconced within a beautiful bay, you will find **Santa Maria Beach** which is a truly enjoyable and tranquil place for swimming and relaxing.

As you travel down the northeastern coast of Sardinia, you'll come across the famous **Emerald Coast**, or *Costa Smeralda* in Italian. This exclusive area was established as such in 1962 by a wealthy group aiming to make a positive impact on the region. Since then, it has become one of the most important and sought-after destinations in Italy. Known for its high-end businesses and luxurious housing and rental properties, it attracts tourists from around the world, making it a popular and prestigious location.

Dotted along this coastline are a number of sophisticated towns where laid-back luxury seems to be the key word. **Liscia di Vacca** is a refined and relaxed area featuring upscale properties which tastefully blend in with the surrounding natural landscape. Adjacent to it is **Porto Cervo**, likely the central hub of the Emerald Coast. Porto Cervo is a sophisticated village boasting its own marina, catering to the affluent with docking facilities for their yachts. The village includes a wealth of designer shops and renowned boutiques, a golf course, art galleries, and refined dining options.

Grande Pevero and **Piccolo Pevero**, situated on either side of a rocky promontory, are true gems along the Emerald Coast.

Below: Grande Pevero at sunset. This 300-metre-long beach is suitable for families with children due to its gently sloping seabed. The picturesque pond of Patima sits at the rear of this exclusive beach. On the following page: a detail of the pink sand in Grande Pevero.

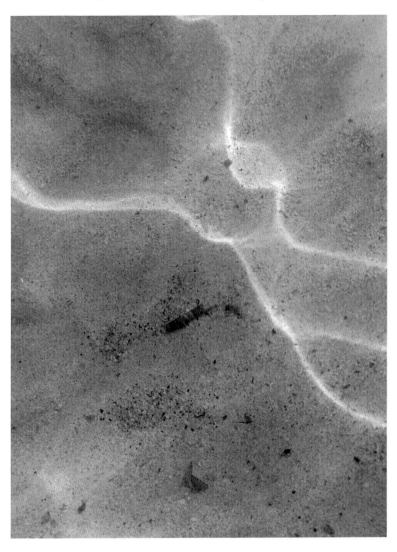

Grande Pevero, the larger beach of the two, has fine white sand and exceptionally clear waters. At its far end, an uneven path over rocky terrain leads to smaller, more secluded coves. For those seeking privacy away from prying eyes, these smaller coves may prove even more enticing than Grande Pevero itself. A further selling point, if it needed one, are the delicately pink streaks of sand which form with the undulating motion of the waves.

On the western side of the promontory which divides the two beaches, lies the smaller twin beach of **Piccolo Pevero**. Surrounded by reddish granite rocks, this cosier beach offers a more intimate setting with less expansive views. Both Grande Pevero and Piccolo Pevero are equipped with numerous amenities, including bars and restaurants, and are complemented by a prestigious golf course nearby.

Rocky terrain to get here - Boat?

Travelling further south brings you to what is arguably the most exquisite beach in the northeastern part of Sardinia, known as **the Prince's Beach** (*Spiaggia del Principe*), so called in honour of an Arab prince in the 60s. Reaching this secluded beach involves a short trek across uneven terrain, requiring a degree of physical prowess to navigate height differences and potentially slippery surfaces. Despite these challenges, the payoff is immense—its waters offer a breathtaking array of blues, sparkling and glistening in a manner that rivals even the most sought-after Caribbean destinations.

On the following page: Looking out to sea from the Prince's beach.

Moving southward, you'll come across a trio of beaches collectively known as **Capriccioli**, each facing a different direction – east, south, and west. Encircled by rounded granite boulders tinged in pale yellow and pale pink, these small bays create a very picturesque setting. In the summer, beaches all across the Emerald Coast area, tend to attract crowds. Nevertheless, their popularity doesn't detract from the enjoyment and overall experience.

Above: Capriccioli on a stormy morning.

Ideal for families, these beaches offer shallow waters, soft sands, and natural wind protection. The predominant hues of the sand range from ochre to yellow, creating a warm and inviting atmosphere. Depending on the direction of the wind, at least one of the three bays will be fully protected, ensuring a peaceful and enjoyable swim.

Heading westward, you'll reach **La Celvia**, a relatively long expanse of sand with a slightly coarser texture, with colours ranging from pale grey to ochre and white.

The diverse composition of the sand results in the sunlight refracting differently off the water in certain places. Situated opposite another stretch of land, La Celvia gives the illusion of being within a lagoon with tranquil, flat waters teeming with fish. The presence of surrounding hills, mountain peaks, and lush vegetation add to the richness of the landscape.

Above: When you visit La Celvia, you get the impression of being in a lagoon. On the following page: Saddled sea bream swim up to people in search of food.

Equipped with a pedalo, boat, or strong swimming skills, you can reach **Elephant Beach** from the northern part of La Celvia. This white sandy cove earned its name from a rock formation shaped by the elements to resemble an elephant.

Continuing southward along the coastline, you'll find yet another beach called **Rena Bianca**, not to be confused with its namesake in the northwest. Rena Bianca boasts fine, white sands, living up to its name (the name means *white sand* in English). With gently sloping shores and shallow waters, it's an ideal spot for families, providing picturesque views over the bay.

Situated on the edge of a promontory, facing Rena Bianca, is the town of **Porto Rotondo**, vying with Porto Cervo as a hub for luxury living and tourism. In this coveted area, you'll find a marina and exquisite high-end residences, complemented by a range of amenities and services, catering to a sophisticated and public lifestyle.

Journey to the southeastern part of this area, to the **Capo Figari promontory.** Here sits the town of **Golfo Aranci**, renowned for its natural charm and beauties. A standout feature is the stunning **Cala Moresca beach**, which provides prime views of **Figarolo Island**, shaped like a triangle and rising directly across from the beach. Easily accessible through a brief and pleasant stroll, this secluded bay is especially peaceful in the early morning.

Above: Cala Moresca on an early summer morning.

In the sea, between Cala Moresca and the island of Figarolo, there's a spot known as **the Dolphins** (*i Delfini*), where dolphin pods make a daily appearance, drawn by the nearby fish farms. From Cala Moresca, you can join dolphin-watching excursions, which give you the chance to paddleboard or kayak alongside these magnificent creatures.

On the following page: Isola Figarolo with its sloping outline.

Dotted around the promontory are several enchanting bays, including **Cala del Sonno**, **Cala Greca**, and **Cala**

Corso, each offering its own distinctive allure.

Head south by car. A 30-minute drive will lead you back to Olbia.

As we come to the end of our journey, we've completed a comprehensive tour of the island, starting and ending in the lively city of Olbia. We hope this guide has provided you with valuable insights and inspiration for your own exploration of this beautiful destination.

❋ ❋ ❋

CONCLUSION

In drawing the final strokes of our journey through Sardinia's landscapes, culture, and coastlines, one can't help but be in awe of what this island offers to every traveller. From the rugged wilderness of Sulcis to the exclusive glamour of the Emerald Coast, Sardinia really has it all.

The island caters to every taste and budget. Its open arms welcome both those in pursuit of opulent indulgence and those embracing the simplicity of sun-kissed shores.

In parting, it beckons as more than a destination; it's an immersive experience, a journey through time and tide. This island is quite a unique place in the Mediterranean—a place that deserves not just to be read about but to be seen, felt, and cherished.

So, pack your curiosity, set sail, and let Sardinia unveil its wonders to you. For in every corner, in each sun-drenched bay and ancient village, there's a piece of the island's soul waiting to be discovered.

*If this book has enhanced your appreciation of Sardinia, fuelled your desire to explore its wonders, or perhaps encouraged a return visit, we invite you to share your experience. **Your reviews are invaluable to us.** Check out our other titles for more similar content. Thank you for joining us on this adventure.*

Amanda and Salvatore

BEST SWIMS IN ITALY

The Best Swims in Italy series is your ultimate guide to discovering the most picturesque beaches across various regions of Italy. The inaugural book, 'Best Swims in Italy - Sardinia Edition,' sets the tone for an immersive journey, curated from the genuine experiences and firsthand accounts of our well-travelled authors. Bringing the beauty of Italy's coastal gems to life, these guides not only provide comprehensive lists but also showcase stunning visuals, capturing the essence of each destination through the skilled lens of our authors. Get ready to explore the finest swims in Italy with a series designed for beach enthusiasts and travel aficionados alike.

Best Swims In Italy - Campania Edition

SOON TO BE RELEASED - Your passport to the finest beaches, bays, and coves across the stunning Campania region in Italy. Immerse yourself in this visual journey and get ready for your next Italian beach adventure.

BOOKS BY THIS AUTHOR

Best Swims In Greece - West Crete Edition

Calling all sun-seekers and sea lovers! If you are craving summer adventures, join us as we explore the crystal-clear waters and breathtaking scenery of picturesque Crete. Discover some of Europe's finest beaches and unlock the secrets of this vibrant island with our comprehensive guide. We'll take you on a tour of the best swimming spots along the stunning coastline of West Crete with "Best Swims in Greece: West Crete Edition." From iconic beaches to secluded coves, this book offers firsthand tips and recommendations from our experienced authors.

Best Swims In Greece - East Crete Edition

SOON TO BE RELEASED - Explore the pristine coastline of East Crete with this comprehensive guide to the region's best beaches and coves. This book offers detailed descriptions, insider tips, and firsthand accounts to help you plan your perfect beach getaway.

Whether you're seeking relaxation or adventure, this guide is your passport to unforgettable seaside experiences in East Crete.